My First Book of
Russian
Words

by Katy R. Kudela

Translator: Translations.com

apple
яблоко
(YAHB-luh-kuh)

CAPSTONE PRESS
a capstone imprint

Table of Contents

How to Use This Dictionary

This book is full of useful words in both Russian and English. The English word appears first, followed by the Russian word. Look below each Russian word for help to sound it out. Try reading the words aloud.

Topic Heading in English

Topic Heading in Russian

Word in English
Word in Russian
(pronunciation)

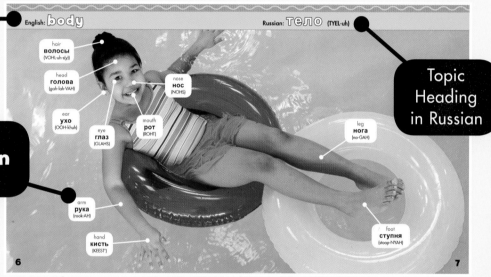

English: **body**

Russian: **тело** (TYEL-uh)

hair
волосы
(VOHL-uh-s(y))

head
голова
(gah-lah-VAH)

ear
ухо
(OOH-khuh)

eye
глаз
(GLAHS)

nose
нос
(NOHS)

mouth
рот
(ROHT)

leg
нога
(na-GAH)

arm
рука
(rook-AH)

hand
кисть
(KEEST')

foot
ступня
(stoop-NYAH)

6

7

Notes about the Russian Language

The Russian language uses a Cyrillic alphabet. This alphabet has 33 letters.

The Russian letter ы does not exist in English. It is shown in this book as (y) and has a vowel sound as "i" in the word "witch."

The Russian letter ь has no sound, but it makes the consonant before it have a soft pronunciaton. It is written as '.

When speaking Russian, some vowels can make the consonant before it soft. Example:

no   **нет**   (NYET)

In the pronunciation (NYET), the letter "y" is used so speakers know to give the consonant "n" a softer sound.

uncle
дядя
(DYA-dyuh)

cousin
двоюродный брат
(dva-YU-rad-nee BRAHT)

mother
мать
(MAHT')

aunt
тётя
(TYO-tyuh)

baby
малыш
(mal-(Y)SH)

Russian: семья (seem'-YAH)

grandmother
бабушка
(BAHB-oosh-kuh)

father
отец
(at-YETS)

grandfather
дедушка
(DYED-oosh-kuh)

brother
брат
(BRAHT)

sister
сестра
(sis-TRAH)

hair
волосы
(VOHL-uh-s(y))

head
голова
(gah-lah-VAH)

ear
ухо
(OOH-khuh)

eye
глаз
(GLAHS)

nose
нос
(NOHS)

mouth
рот
(ROHT)

arm
рука
(rook-AH)

hand
кисть
(KEEST')

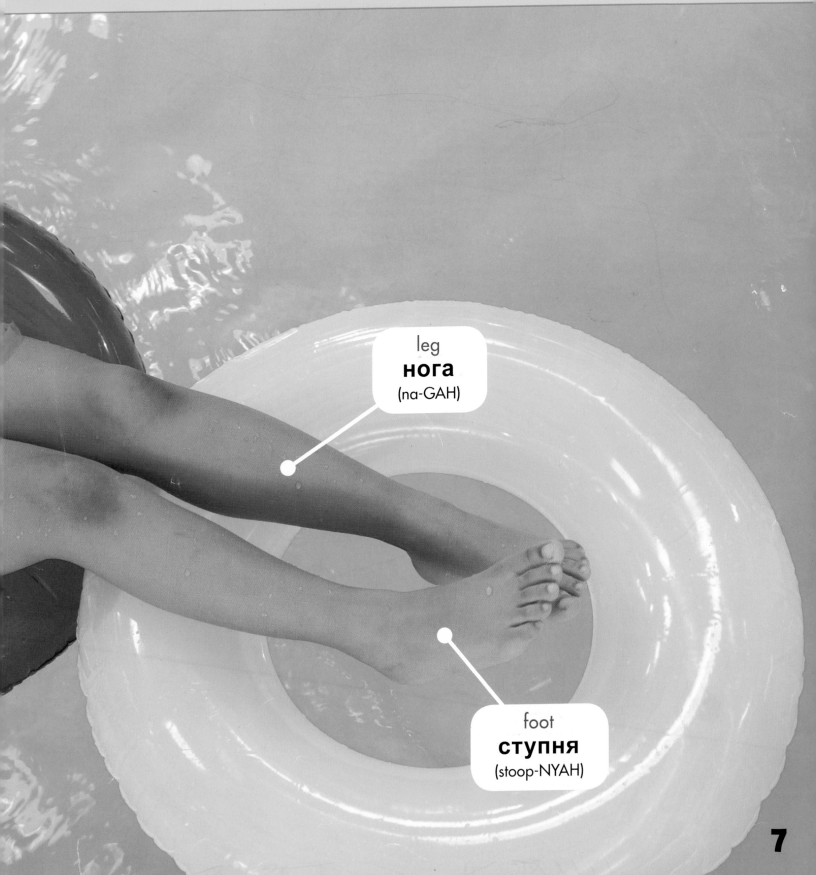

leg
нога
(na-GAH)

foot
ступня
(stoop-NYAH)

pajamas
пижама
(pee-ZHAH-muh)

coat
пальто
(pal'-TOH)

shorts
шорты
(SHORT-(y))

boot
сапог
(sa-POK)

8

shoe
ботинок
(ba-TEEN-uhk)

hat
шапка
(SHAHP-kuh)

pants
штаны
(shtahn-(Y))

sock
носок
(na-SOHK)

dress
платье
(PLAHT'-yeh)

shirt
рубашка
(roo-BAHSH-kuh)

9

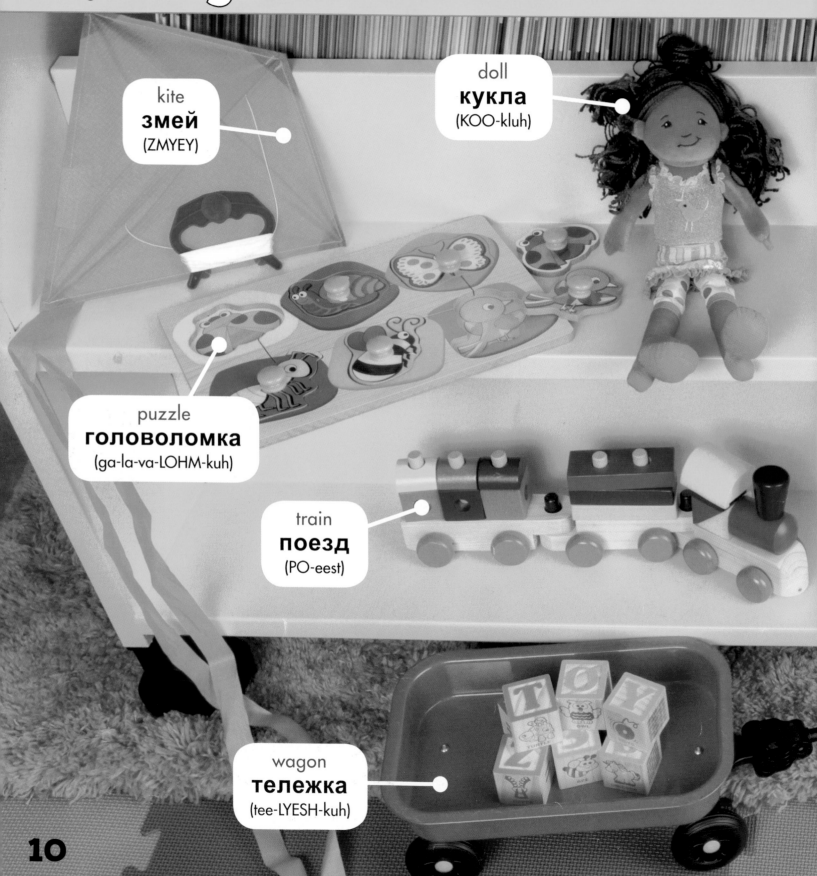

kite
змей
(ZMYEY)

doll
кукла
(KOO-kluh)

puzzle
головоломка
(ga-la-va-LOHM-kuh)

train
поезд
(PO-eest)

wagon
тележка
(tee-LYESH-kuh)

puppet
марионетка
(ma-ree-uh-NYET-kuh)

skateboard
скейтборд
(SKAYT-bort)

jump rope
скакалка
(ska-KAHL-kuh)

ball
мяч
(MYACH)

bat
бита
(BEE-tah)

11

picture
картина
(kar-TEEN-uh)

lamp
лампа
(LAHM-puh)

window
окно
(ak-NOH)

dresser
комод
(ka-MOHT)

curtain
занавеска
(za-nuh-VYES-kuh)

blanket
одеяло
(ah-dee-YAH-luh)

12

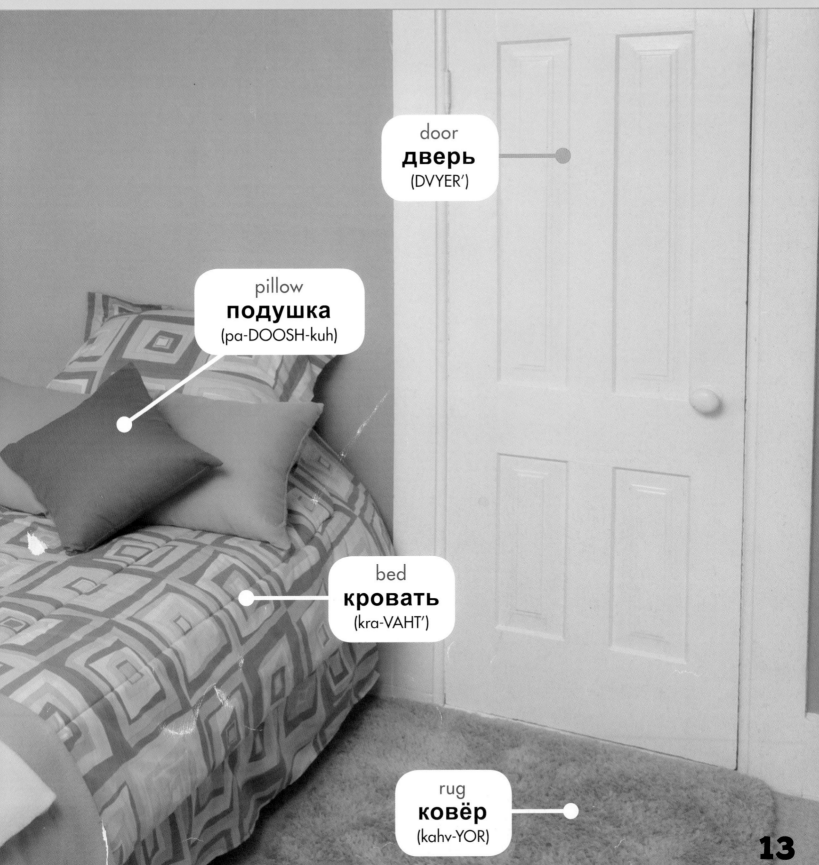

door
дверь
(DVYER')

pillow
подушка
(pa-DOOSH-kuh)

bed
кровать
(kra-VAHT')

rug
ковёр
(kahv-YOR)

bathtub
ванна
(VAHN-nuh)

soap
мыло
(M(Y)L-uh)

toilet
унитаз
(oon-ee-TAHZ)

14

mirror
зеркало
(ZYER-ka-luh)

toothbrush
зубная щётка
(zoob-NAH-yuh SHCHOT-kuh)

toothpaste
зубная паста
(zoob-NAH-yuh PAHST-uh)

comb
расчёска
(ras-CHOHS-kuh)

sink
раковина
(RAH-kuh-vee-nuh)

towel
полотенце
(pa-la-TYEN-tsuh)

brush
щётка
(SHCHOT-kuh)

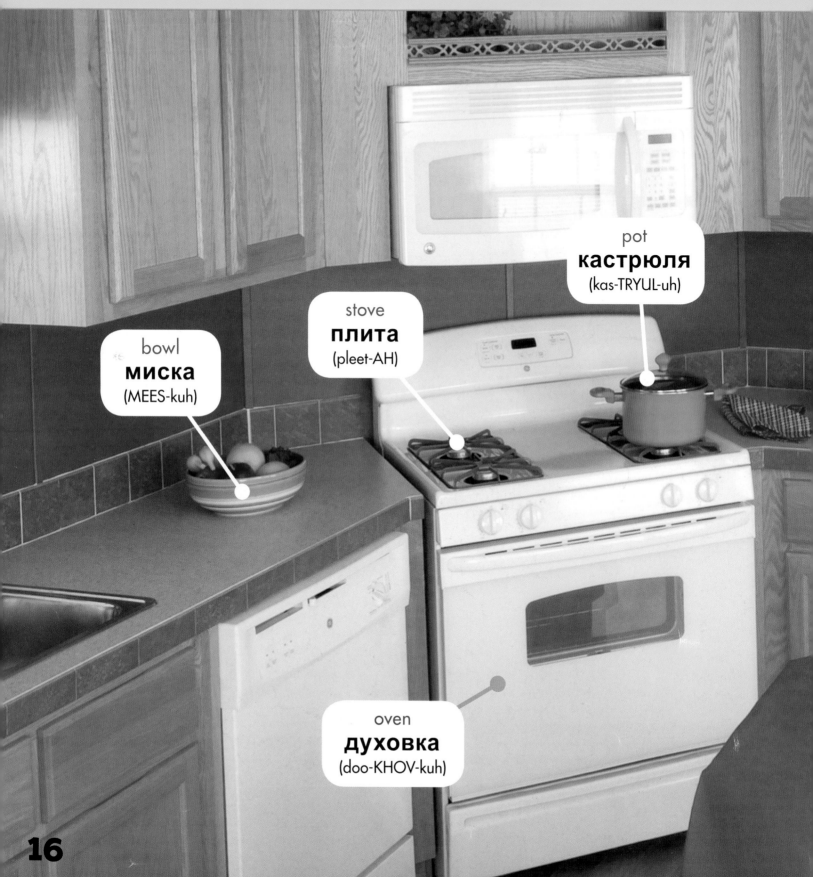

pot
кастрюля
(kas-TRYUL-uh)

stove
плита
(pleet-AH)

bowl
миска
(MEES-kuh)

oven
духовка
(doo-KHOV-kuh)

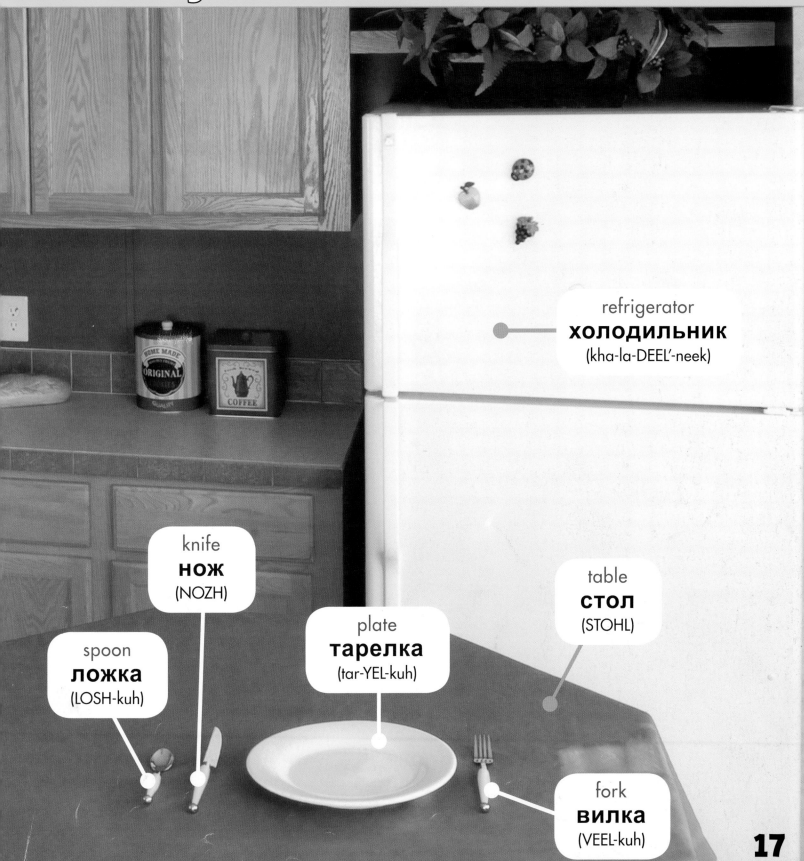

refrigerator
холодильник
(kha-la-DEEL'-neek)

knife
нож
(NOZH)

table
стол
(STOHL)

spoon
ложка
(LOSH-kuh)

plate
тарелка
(tar-YEL-kuh)

fork
вилка
(VEEL-kuh)

17

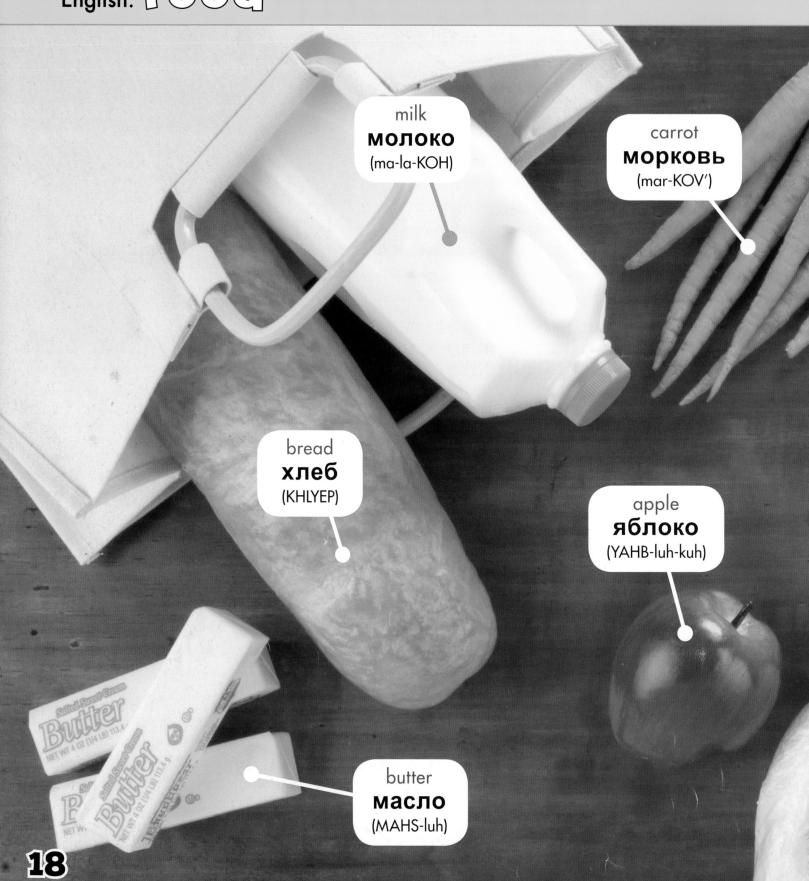

milk
молоко
(ma-la-KOH)

carrot
морковь
(mar-KOV')

bread
хлеб
(KHLYEP)

apple
яблоко
(YAHB-luh-kuh)

butter
масло
(MAHS-luh)

egg
яйцо
(yee-TSOH)

pea
горох
(ga-ROKH)

orange
апельсин
(ah-pel'-SEEN)

sandwich
бутерброд
(boot-uhr-BROT)

rice
рис
(REES)

tractor
трактор
(TRAK-tuhr)

hay
сено
(SYEH-nuh)

fence
забор
(za-BOR)

farmer
фермер
(FYER-mer)

sheep
овца
(av-TSAH)

pig
свинья
(sveen'-YAH)

horse
лошадь
(LOH-shad')

barn
хлев
(KHLYEF)

cow
корова
(kar-OHV-uh)

chicken
курица
(KOOR-ee-tsah)

21

leaf
лист
(LEEST)

butterfly
бабочка
(BAHB-uch-kuh)

flower
цветок
(tsvee-TOHK)

shovel
совок
(sah-VOHK)

bird
птица
(PTEE-tsuh)

worm
червяк
(cher-VYAHK)

plant
растение
(ras-TYEN-ee-yuh)

grass
трава
(tra-VAH)

dirt
земля
(zeem-LYAH)

seed
семя
(SYEM-yuh)

Edamame Green Soybean
Tohya

$2.99
Net Weight
15 grams

80 days
Warm season
crop - plant after
last chance of
spring frost

So high in
protein, it is
called "the meat
without bones".
Boiled, beans
are popped out
of the pod into
your mouth for
a culinary
delight!

23

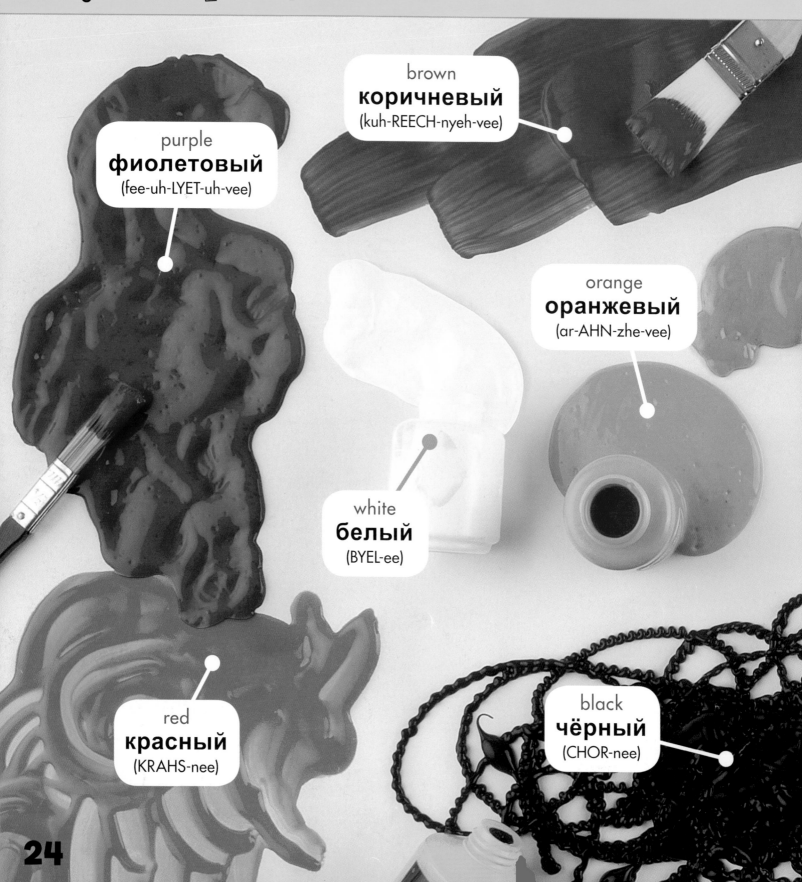

brown
коричневый
(kuh-REECH-nyeh-vee)

purple
фиолетовый
(fee-uh-LYET-uh-vee)

orange
оранжевый
(ar-AHN-zhe-vee)

white
белый
(BYEL-ee)

red
красный
(KRAHS-nee)

black
чёрный
(CHOR-nee)

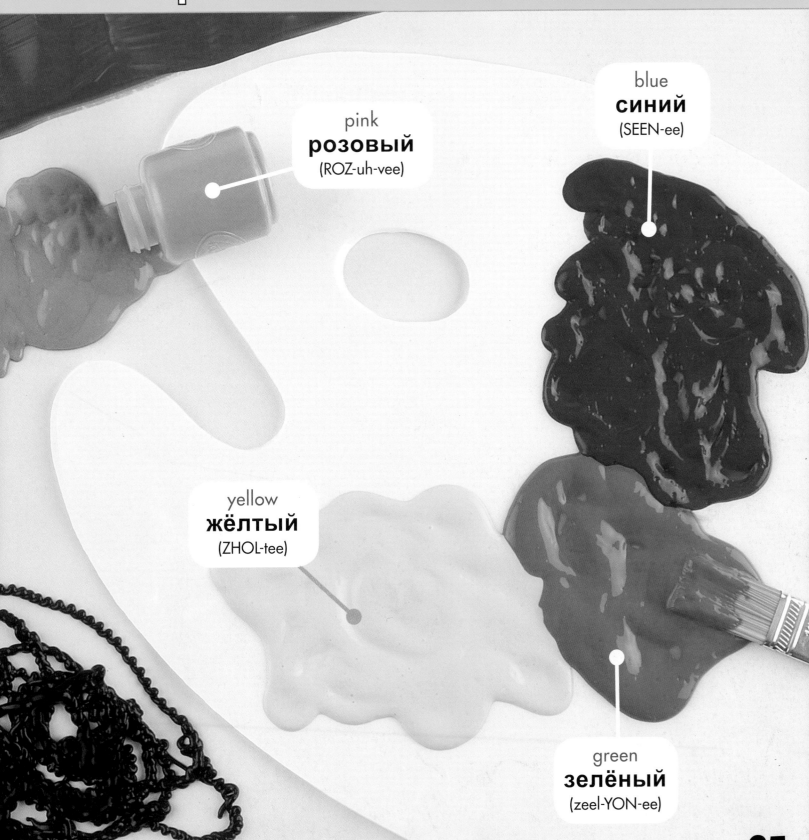

pink
розовый
(ROZ-uh-vee)

blue
синий
(SEEN-ee)

yellow
жёлтый
(ZHOL-tee)

green
зелёный
(zeel-YON-ee)

teacher
учительница
(oo-CHEE-tel'-nee-tsuh)

book
книга
(kuh-NEE-guh)

desk
стол
(STOHL)

pencil
карандаш
(ka-ran-DAHSH)

crayon
цветной карандаш
(tsveet-NOY ka-ran-DAHSH)

26

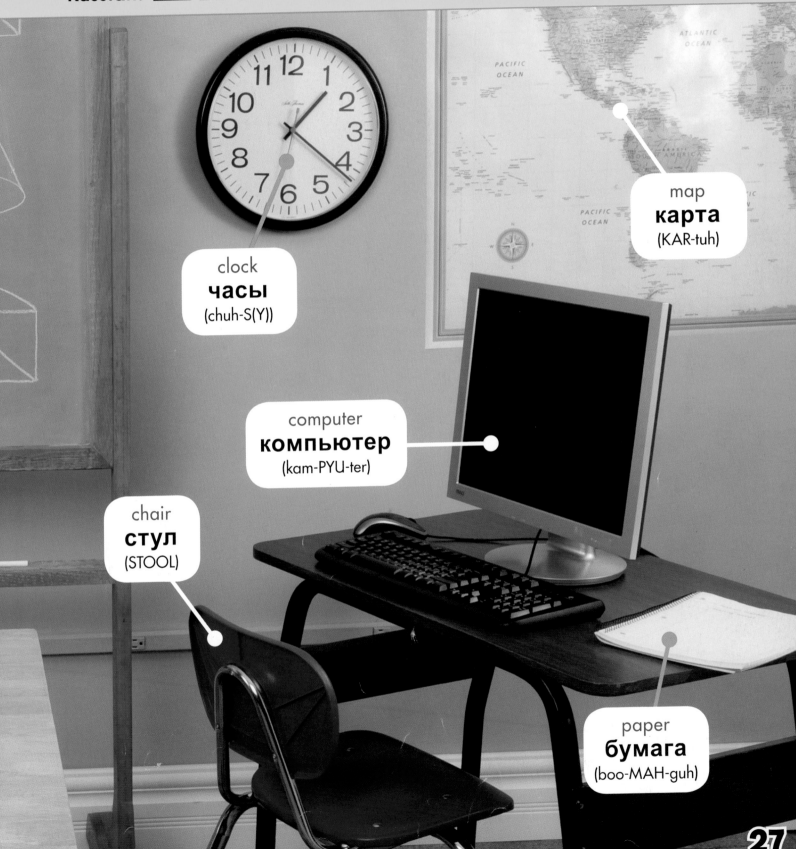

map
карта
(KAR-tuh)

clock
часы
(chuh-S(Y))

computer
компьютер
(kam-PYU-ter)

chair
стул
(STOOL)

paper
бумага
(boo-MAH-guh)

traffic light
светофор
(svyet-uh-FOHR)

library
библиотека
(bee-blee-uh-TYEK-uh)

store
магазин
(ma-ga-ZEEN)

LIBRARY

ONE WAY

Tuesday 2:00-5:00
Thursday 2:00-6:00

bicycle
велосипед
(vee-luh-see-PYET)

car
машина
(ma-SHEEN-uh)

tree
дерево
(DYER-ee-vuh)

bus
автобус
(af-TOH-boos)

park
парк
(PARK)

street
улица
(OOL-ee-tsuh)

sign
знак
(ZNAHK)

STOP

29

Numbers • **Числа** (CHEES-luh)

1. one • **один** (ahd-EEN)
2. two • **два** (DVAH)
3. three • **три** (TREE)
4. four • **четыре** (chee-T(Y)-ree)
5. five • **пять** (PYAT')

6. six • **шесть** (SHYEST')
7. seven • **семь** (SYEM')
8. eight • **восемь** (VO-sem')
9. nine • **девять** (DYEV-yet')
10. ten • **десять** (DYES-yet')

Useful Phrases • **Полезные фразы** (pa-LYEZ-nee-eh FRAH-Z(Y))

yes • **да** (DAH)

no • **нет** (NYET)

hello • **привет** (pri-VYET)

good-bye • **до свидания** (da-svee-DAHN-yuh)

good morning • **доброе утро** (DOH-bree OO-truh)

good night • **спокойной ночи** (spa-KOY-nee NOH-chee)

please • **пожалуйста** (pah-ZHAHL-oos-tuh)

thank you • **спасибо** (spa-SEE-buh)

excuse me • **извините** (iz-veen-EE-tyeh)

My name is _____. • **Меня зовут** _____. (meen-YA zah-VOOT)

30

Read More

Amery, Heather. *First Thousand Words in Russian.* London: Usborne Books, 2005.

Mahoney, Judy. *Teach Me—Everyday Russian.* Teach Me—Minnetonka, Minn.: Teach Me Tapes, 2008.

Turhan, Sedat. *Milet Picture Dictionary: English-Russian.* Chicago: Milet Publishing, 2003.

Internet Sites

FactHound offers a safe, fun way to find Internet sites related to this book. All of the sites on FactHound have been researched by our staff.

Here's all you do:

Visit *www.facthound.com*

FactHound will fetch the best sites for you!

A+ Books are published by Capstone Press,
151 Good Counsel Drive, P.O. Box 669, Mankato, Minnesota 56002.
www.capstonepress.com

092009
005620LKS10

 Books published by Capstone Press are manufactured with paper
containing at least 10 percent post-consumer waste.

Library of Congress Cataloging-in-Publication Data
Kudela, Katy R.
    My first book of Russian words / by Katy R. Kudela.
    p. cm. — (A+ books. Bilingual picture dictionaries)
    Includes bibliographical references.
    Summary: "Simple text paired with themed photos invite the reader to learn to speak
Russian" — Provided by publisher.
    ISBN 978-1-4296-3917-0 (library binding)
    1. Picture dictionaries, Russian — Juvenile literature. 2. Picture dictionaries,
English — Juvenile literature. 3. Russian language — Dictionaries, Juvenile — English.
4. English language — Dictionaries, Juvenile — Russian. I. Title.
PE1129.R8K83 2010
491.73'21 — dc22   2009028664

Credits
Juliette Peters, designer; Wanda Winch, media researcher; Laura Manthe, production specialist

Photo Credits
Capstone Studio/Gary Sundermeyer, cover (pig), 20 (farmer with tractor, pig)
Capstone Studio/Karon Dubke, cover (ball, sock), back cover (toothbrush), 1, 3,
    4–5, 6–7, 8–9, 10–11, 12–13, 14–15, 16–17, 18–19, 22–23, 24–25, 26–27
Image Farm, back cover, 1, 2, 31, 32 (design elements)
iStockphoto/Andrew Gentry, 28 (main street)
Photodisc, cover (flower)
Shutterstock/Adrian Matthiassen, cover (butterfly); David Hughes, 20 (hay); Eric Isselee,
    20–21 (horse); hamurishi, 28 (bike); Ievgeniia Tikhonova, 21 (chickens); Jim Mills, 29
    (stop sign); Kelli Westfal, 28 (traffic light); Margo Harrison, 20 (sheep); MaxPhoto, 21
    (cow and calf); Melinda Fawver, 29 (bus); Robert Elias, 20–21 (barn, fence); Vladimir
    Mucibabic, 28–29 (city skyline)

Note to Parents, Teachers, and Librarians
Learning to speak a second language at a young age has been shown to improve overall
academic performance, boost problem-solving ability, and foster an appreciation for other
cultures. Early exposure to language skills provides a strong foundation for other subject
areas, including math and reasoning. Introducing children to a second language can help
to lay the groundwork for future academic success and cultural awareness.